W9-BEW-766

WORDS AT
WORK

WORDS AT WORK

An insider's guide to the language of professions

Mim Harrison

Illustrations by Lee Passarella

Walker & Company
New York

Published by Walker Publishing Company, Inc., New York
Distributed to the trade by Holtzbrinck Publishers

All papers used by Walker & Company are natural, recyclable products made from wood grown in well-managed forests. The manufacturing processes conform to the environmental regulations of the country of origin.

Library of Congress Cataloging-in-Publication Data has been applied for.

ISBN-10: 0-8027-1568-0
ISBN-13: 978-0-8027-1568-5

Visit Walker & Company's Web site at www.walkerbooks.com

First published with the title *Spoken Like a Pro* by Levenger Press in 2006
Published in hardcover by Walker & Company in 2007

1 3 5 7 9 10 8 6 4 2

Book design by Danielle Furci
Printed in the United States of America by Quebecor World Taunton

For Mrs. Wehmeyer,

on behalf of all the students

who learned from you

the language of thought and ideas.

And for my father,

who taught me how to be

a true professional.

Contents

Contents

Contents

Preface

Match the expression at left with the correct profession at right.

___ 1. Squatter	a.	Cookie baker
___ 2. Barking	b.	Airline pilot
___ 3. Bug smasher	c.	Broadway company manager
___ 4. Penny stacking	d.	Retailer
___ 5. Double counter	e.	Venture capitalist
___ 6. Tag	f.	Hairdresser
___ 7. City ledger	g.	Television promo producer
___ 8. Gang up	h.	Perfume maker
___ 9. Licorice sticks	i.	Hotelier
___ 10. Hockey stick	j.	Restaurateur
___ 11. Tipping fee	k.	Pharmacist
___ 12. Pucks	l.	Printer
___ 13. Hardwood	m.	Microbiologist
___ 14. Splicing & dicing	n.	Waste manager
___ 15. Miser's dream	o.	Symphony orchestra musician
___ 16. Torn & tattered	p.	Magician

Answers are in the book.

(If you're really in a hurry, go to the Final Word.)

Introduction

Samuel Johnson called them cant words and didn't think much of them. The great eighteenth-century lexicographer, who once defined himself as "a writer of dictionaries, a harmless drudge," found words exclusive to a profession to be on a par with "formal affected language" and the kind of talk delivered in "a peculiar and studied tone of voice."

So why devote a book to the prose of the pros? If language is meant to facilitate communication, don't words accessible to only a select few impede it? If only certain engineers know why FONSI doesn't matter, how does that help the rest of us? ✻

But there's another way to look at these terms. Fast foods, interstates, chain stores— they've conspired to make us all alike. Yet most of us delight in knowing that a New Yorker calls that frothy soda fountain drink a milkshake, a Bostonian knows it as a frappe and a Rhode Islander refers to it

Milkshake/frappe/cabinet

Introduction

as a cabinet. Professionspeak may be one of the few other regionalisms left in America, albeit not one of geography.

There is a special satisfaction in coming upon a term such as tin knocker and knowing that it is the name industrial plumbers assign to the sheet-metal workers installing the ductwork. Or understanding that when a lobbyist says that the legislators are going to take a walk, it means they're leaving the committee room because they've decided not to vote on a particular issue. Or decoding a police officer's reference to felony flyers as high-priced sneakers.

"People love to read about work," observed Stephen King in *On Writing*. "God knows why, but they do." Perhaps because so many of us have to, or want to, or used to, or hope to work. Listen to the opening lines between two strangers: one of the most frequently asked questions is, "And what do you do?" If we define ourselves in part by what we do, why not define the special vocabularies that help us do it?

Interestingly, even the pros caution that within their fields, the terminology can differ from one place to another, one organization to another. A police dispatch signal in one jurisdiction does not necessarily indicate the same activity in another. One restaurant kitchen may shout "Order up!" to the server while another will announce "The slide is full." (Either way, the food for table seven is ready.) Tip O'Neill's famous maxim about all politics being local holds true for the lexicon of a profession, too.

Conversely, some expressions cross professions. Both a magician and a Broadway actor understand what it means to perform, or act, in one, because they both work from a stage. But who would guess that a venture capitalist and a microbiologist share the term hockey stick, even though each uses it differently?

This chameleon quality of English is among the many traits that make our language so vigorous. "It is the most capacious vital tongue of all," exulted Walt Whitman, "an enormous treasure house...chock full of so many contributions."

No doubt Whitman did not have dribble board, dummy juice and wand wagger in mind when he wrote that. But the language of work is among those many contributions.

Introduction

Professional shorthand packs an abundance of meaning and information into one crisp, efficient word or phrase.

Perhaps this fascination with working words is part of America's independent streak. As Stacy Schiff tells us in her biography of Benjamin Franklin, the perspicacious patriot advised those Europeans who contemplated moving across the pond after the American Revolution to check their inherited titles at the door. In America,

Felony flyers

explained Franklin (who had been a printer's apprentice by the age of twelve), "people do not enquire concerning a stranger, *what is he?* but *what can he do?*"

Here, then, are some of the curious, oddball, unexpected and useful words that professionals put to work.

⁂ *FONSI is an acronym used in engineering for Finding Of No Significant Impact.*

"Eighty-six on the fillets"

(Restaurateur)

"Food comes first, then morals," pronounces a character in Bertolt Brecht's *Threepenny Opera*. The connection with theater is apt. "Curtain up" is how one restaurant pro describes the act of opening a restaurant to the public every day. And there is often plenty of high drama between the front of the house—the maître d', servers, runners and bussers—and the back, with both the lowly dishwasher and the lofty chef.

Four-top. The customer hears "table for four," but in restaurant parlance that's a four-top. A one-top is called a solo or an ace. A two-top is a deuce.

Over the top. Nothing to do with table count. It's a guest who's had too much to drink.

Green table. Vegetarians.

"I need to turn table eleven." When you turn a table,

you get another seating from it. Turning tables is good for the bottom line.

"You have a squatter at sixteen." The words a maître d' hates to hear from the servers. Squatters (or campers) are guests who overstay their welcome, thus diminishing the maître d's chances of turning their table. Restaurants calculate an average time for guests to be at a table. Depending on the type of restaurant, a two-top could mean a stay of an hour and a quarter; a four-top, an hour and a half; a five-top, easily two hours.

Green table

HM. High-maintenance table. Servers and hosts usually quickly determine who the most demanding guests are.

"I'm getting slammed." What one server moans to another when the host seats the server's section all at one time. A server whose section includes a lot of view tables, such as the tables by the windows, is often the most vulnerable. "I got doubled" is a comparable lament, occurring when two of the server's tables are "sat" at the same time.

Dropping the food. Not to worry: this doesn't describe the wait staff's dropping the steaming bowl of bouillabaisse on your lap. Dropping the food, in this context, means delivering it to the table. The runner confirms to the server: "I just dropped seven," meaning, the group at table seven has just been served. ❈

Runner. Have you noticed that the person who drops your food is not always the same person who took your order? The runner is the delivery person. Runners help full-service restaurants get more mileage from their servers, who are seen as the salespeople. The longer you can legitimately keep servers on the floor, the greater the possibility of their upselling drinks, desserts and other pricey items.

"Fire the app." Start preparing the appetizer in the kitchen.

"Order in." A server's announcement to the kitchen that he or she has just placed an order.

"I need a swordfish 9-1-1 at table twelve." Also known as calling an order to the kitchen. You hear it when the server forgets to include the dish in the initial order and now needs it pronto.

Call a rush. A maître d' does this on a busy night when a table could be turned if the customers could get their order faster. The kitchen pulls the ticket, or order, for that table forward in the queue.

Call the drinks. How a server places an order with the bartender. These days, computers do most of the calling, but in old-school bars and restaurants, it's still the server. Etiquette requires that the server wait until the bartender makes eye contact and calls him or her by name. Then the server calls the drinks in a specific sequence, depending on how the house sets up the bar. One scenario might be: ups (martini), neats (Scotch, no ice), rocks (Scotch with ice), highballs (gin and tonic), blendeds (frozen daiquiri). The server also calls the liquors in a specific sequence, such as: vodka, gin, rum, bourbon, Scotch, brandy. These protocols keep the bar running efficiently even on busy nights, since all the staff is following the same drill.

Mise en place. Pronounced "meez-on-PLOSS," it's a

Restaurateur

French term that literally means "put in place," and it's how chefs plan ahead. Watch some of those cooking shows and see how all the ingredients are measured, chopped and ready for the chef to grab as he or she prepares the dish. That's *mise en place*. In busy kitchens, the pace is hectic, and being able to reach quickly for everything you need helps the chef keep pace.

Servers have their own version of *mise en place*—when they mark the table with dessert spoons, for example, or prep a condiment caddy.

"I only work the dupes." This is not something a chef *says*. It's what a chef *growls* to servers who ask for food they haven't written on the tickets.

Often a chef works from the duplicate copy of that ticket. Chefs can't read

'I need a swordfish 9-1-1'

minds (grumble grumble). They read only dupes. It's not a thing till you ring the order into the computer so that a dupe comes up.

"Give me an all-day on the burgers." It's more efficient to grill seven hamburgers at one time than to grill them one at a time. A chef will ask to see all the tickets that have the same menu item. It's not really an all-day list, however—just all the comparable menu items at any given point in the day.

Call the drinks

"The slide is full." The code for servers who are on the floor to return to the kitchen and pick up the orders that are ready. Once the chef prepares an order, the plate goes to a separate part of the kitchen called the slide, where an expediter hands off the finished plates to the server or runner. Depending on how big and how fancy the restaurant, adding the finishing touches of garnish may be the job of the chef, the sous chef or the expediter.

Restaurateur

Another way to announce that the slide is full is to call out "Section two, order up." That cues the server who's handling section two that an order is ready.

"I'm on my wings." What servers say to the kitchen when they need to get the food to the table pronto.

Eighty-six. When the kitchen calls out this number about a specific dish, it means they've temporarily run out of it. It's a dead menu item, as far as there being any prepped, so "eighty-six on the fillets." One theory about the origin of the expression: an open grave is eight feet long and six feet deep.

Sixty-eight. The dish that was eighty-sixed is on again because the kitchen has been able to prep some more. So "sixty-eight on the filet mignons."

Breaking down the plates. Lowly though dishwashers may be, they have their limits, too. So bussers bringing in dirty dishes are instructed to break them down, or separate them, before they drop them (not literally, of course). Glassware gets separated from plates, straws get thrown in the trash, and so on.

"A clean kitchen is a slow kitchen." Try this line at home the next time you've dirtied every pan, knife and cutting board to sauté two mushrooms. If a restaurant's kitchen is clean during open hours, it's cursed. It means there's a dearth of guests.

GI. Off-hours, you better believe that kitchen is clean. About once a week, a restaurant undergoes a general inspection, or GI, giving the whole place a thorough scouring.

"Time to lean, time to clean." A kitchen worker who's just hanging around may hear this from the boss. If there's time to lean against the wall, there's time to clean.

Cover the nut. Cover your expenses. A restaurant requires a minimum number of orders each day to cover its nut, or break even. If you need to pull in $4,000 a day and the average price of a meal is $28, you need 143 orders to break even.

Whale. A fat tipper, one who leaves more than twenty percent.

Stiff. A table that leaves less than fifteen percent.

Restaurateur

"They must be European." Guests who tip less than ten percent. (In Europe, the gratuity is usually included in the bill.)

❋ Footnote to dropping the food:

How do runners usually know who gets the baked scrod and who ordered the tenderloin medium rare? Most restaurants use a pivot point method, counting off seat numbers from the agreed-upon approach point at a table. At a four-top, for example, the first seat to the left of the server's approach point is seat 1. The numbers then go clockwise, ending at seat 4, on the server's right. The servers write these numbers on each ticket, or code them into the computer. The information is then available to the runners.

Poodles and cannibals

(Retailer)

Could shopping be a sign of some latent tribal behavior? If the language of retail is any indication, it comes close to being a basic animal instinct: canine lexicon runs wild throughout retail-speak.

Store dog. Many retailers who have survived for more than fifteen years refer to themselves as store dogs. Think head office vs. stores, officer vs. infantry: those working dogs in the stores are the ones fetching and retrieving and working like dogs.

Barking. There was a time that, inspired by the circus barkers from the Big Top, retailers in places like New York set up high chairs outside their stores, "barking" to passersby to come in. The music that lures you into—or repels you from—many of today's mall stores is barking up the same tree.

"It dogged." The product didn't sell. To de-dog it, retailers reset the merchandise: they change the display or the product's position in the store.

Poodle traffic. Your slave-to-fashion customers. One store dog explained that poodles come in different breeds. The wannabe poodle has more attitude than money. The diamond-stud poodle has both. "At retail," this industry wag told us, "the earrings are the giveaway. Big diamonds tell it all."

Poodle traffic

No resistance. What store dogs drool over. Diamond-stud poodles have no resistance—they don't blink an eye at the price. Such high-toned shoppers are part of the carriage trade. The term harks back to the genteel days when wealthy society ladies arrived at stores in their horse-drawn carriages, often with their maids in tow and their coachmen double-parked.

Sight line. What *don't* you see when you walk into a store? Most of us don't see the bottom shelves of fixtures; we see only around eye level. Poor sight line is similar to the blind spot in a car mirror. Stores merchandise, or display, their wares to avoid a poor sight line. Grocery stores have their own maxim for it: "Eye level is buy level."

Planogram. A detailed layout of a selling floor. Planograms explain why you find the same brand displayed the same way in different stores.

Hard lines, soft lines. Hard lines, or hard goods, is an umbrella term for all home products such as furniture. Soft lines, or soft goods, are textiles. Note that a rug can be soft as down but it's still a hard line because it's for the home.

Open sell. As close as a store comes to saying "help yourself." The merchandise is on the racks and the counters, for you to touch and test, without needing a salesperson to open cabinets or go in the back room to find more.

"Pile it high, watch it fly." Also known as commodity selling, it's stacking the merchandise on the fixture, then signing it with a compelling price point in the hope that customers buy the stuff like crazy. (Signing is a short way of saying "creating a sign," while price point is a long way of saying "price.")

Turn & burn. A close cousin to high & fly. To sell a

product quickly, retailers mass it out with a big display. The store could either be desperate or capitalizing on a popular item that's well stocked. In that case, a retailer might say, "This item is so hot, we're just turning and burning."

Attachment rate. The success of a product is often enhanced by the number of additional sales you can attach to it. About to buy a laptop? Let's see if I can sell you a travel case, a portable mouse, surge protector, full-size keyboard...and the list continues. These add-ons give the laptop a high attachment rate.

In-stock position. If you have enough of a product for every customer who wants to buy it, you have great in-stock position. And it's no accident: retailers use it as a strategy for ratcheting up sales on promotional merchandise as well as on basic commodities—the core items that your customers always expect you to have in stock.

Trendy merchandise, on the other hand, doesn't need this strategy: you want to sell it quickly, while it's still hot.

Walking business. A way of saying you've lost the sale because you didn't have the goods the customers wanted. Or at least what they *thought* they wanted. A good salesperson won't let 'em walk but trades them up instead.

Trading up. Offering customers better or more expensive items than the ones they were originally looking for. Trade those customers up and you just may keep them from walking.

Spiff. Spiff programs are financial incentives that manufacturers or retailers implement to help a product sell better. "Let's spiff it," they say, and they give the sales staff a buck or more for every product the salespeople sell. Usually the more expensive the product, the higher the spiff, so the more money for the sales staff. The term harks back to the 1890s and the textile trade. But even the *Oxford English Dictionary* scratches its head as to the word's beginnings, admitting it's "of obscure origin."

Popping 'em. Selling a product quickly at a particular price point. "We've been poppin' these lamps for one-fifty," a happy retailer might say (meaning one hundred fifty dollars).

BOGO. Buy One, Get One. A common ruse in promotions or to move excess inventory, the offer is one that many shoppers can't resist, as it often means getting two items for the price of one. GWP, or Gift With Purchase, is a staple of cosmetics promotions and the reason so many women seem to have forty-two cosmetic bags. With a PWP, or Purchase With Purchase, one product is discounted when linked to the purchase of another. This makes the customer happy and also moves more inventory, which makes the retailer happy.

Outposting. Let's say a store normally displays briefcases among its leather goods. With the approach of Father's Day, the salespeople might decide to display some of the stock in a swing area—a part of the selling floor that can be used for different purposes depending on the season.

Such an outpost gives strong sellers well-timed additional visibility. By having those briefcases in two places on the selling floor, the odds increase that shoppers will buy them.

MAP. The acronym for minimum advertised price, which the manufacturer establishes. To encourage retailers to charge MAP, a manufacturer might offer the stores financial support, or co-op money, for their advertising.

Keystone. Inventory that's keystoned has a fifty percent markup: the retail price is twice the wholesale cost.

Words At Work

One to show, one to go. A selling tactic when retailers want to be cautious with inventory investment. They keep only one unit on the selling floor, for show, and only one in the stockroom, for go. When it goes, the retailer may then reorder to replenish stock.

"It's on wheels." The inventory is returnable to the manufacturer if it dogs at retail.

SAD. The way retailers feel when they have to hold a Scratch-And-Dent event (aka sale).

SKU. The acronym for stock-keeping unit, pronounced *skew*. Retailers assign a SKU as a way of tracking inventory. An item may have several SKUs—one for each size and color of a sweater, for instance. The total number of SKUs a retailer keeps is one measure of the business's complexity.

"Retail is detail." As in SKUs and other mind-numbing details. Just in case you thought it was all fun.

Cannibalized sales. When one product detracts from the sale of a comparable one, you've cannibalized your sales. Retail really is a dog-eat-dog world.

Greasers, eepers and glory

(Airline Pilot)

Listen closely to airplane argot and if you weren't in the air, you might think you were on the seas. Pilots refer to their aircrafts as ships; when calling Maintenance, they're often asked, "What's your ship number?" Passengers distinguish one side of the plane from the other by seat letters, but flight crews refer to port and starboard. Pilots measure their air speed in knots and steer their planes, when they're on the ground, with a tiller. (Contrary to popular belief, computers don't totally fly the aircraft. Pilots generally control takeoffs, approaches and landings by hand. They use autopilots during the "cruise" portion of the flight—similar to the cruise control in cars.)

Power back. The way to get a smaller airliner, such as a DC-9 or 727, into reverse when it's leaving the gate is to power it back. The power comes not from the wheels but from redirecting the jet blast, or thrust of the engines.

Words At Work

Larger planes rely on **tugs** to maneuver them away from the gate (that nautical influence again). These are the little blue tractors that give a mighty push or pull: they're filled with concrete and counterbalanced. The tug first pushes the plane away from the gate. Then if needed, it pulls it away from a crowded ramp to a safe distance for starting the engine.

Full-route clearance. You're taxiing toward the runway for takeoff and it looked as though you were going to take off from *this* direction but now it looks as though it's *that* way instead. The tower—Air Traffic Control—has just given your pilot a whole new set of departure directions. The proper response from the cockpit is never "Roger." Instead, the pilot must read back the entire clearance to the controller.

Hold short. It may seem as though you're on that runway forever as the plane snakes around, preparing to take off. But most of that tarmac is made up of **taxiways** and **ramps.** Aircraft spend minimal time on the runway itself, and they hold short of the runway until it's their turn—meaning, they stop short of the runway until they're cleared for takeoff.

Airline Pilot

Eeper. The proper way to pronounce EPR, for Exhaust Pressure Ratio, a way to measure engine power.

Cross-check. You've heard it on nearly every takeoff (even if you weren't listening): "Flight attendants, prepare for cross-check." The pilot or copilot is instructing the crew to double-check each other's door to ensure it's properly closed.

A checklist accompanies every phase of a flight: starting the engines, taxiing, takeoff, after-takeoff climb, cruising, descent, landing, after landing and parking.

Jump seat. The seat in the cockpit that an instructor or check pilot uses when observing the crew. It's also the seat that a pilot who's not flying the aircraft can use when hitching a ride to a destination. As one veteran high-altitude hitchhiker advises, comfortable it's not.

Flying sideways. The way that the flight engineer, or FE, used to fly. Not literally, of course. But back when the FAA required an FE in the cockpit, the FE faced sideways rather than forward (except during takeoff and landing). FEs did what computers now do; managing the electric systems, computing engine power setting and getting weather data were among the myriad tasks. The instrument panels and gauges were mounted on the side of the cockpit, so the FE flew facing them, or sideways.

Pax. Passengers.

Indian Country. Some of the smaller private planes made by the Piper Corporation have names such as Apache, Navajo, Comanche and Cheyenne. They fly low and slow compared with airliners, usually below 10,000 feet and 250 knots. This is Indian Country, and not where a commercial jetliner wants to be.

Bug smasher. Another swipe at low-flying, light aircraft such as the Piper and Cessna. Presumably they fly so low, they share air space with insects.

Weather. Have you noticed that airline personnel almost never talk about *bad* weather? You're simply "experiencing some weather." This is to prevent the pax from fretting about the prospects of experiencing snow, ice, sleet, hail, thunder, lightning and other weather.

Airline Pilot

Glazing. Talk about weather—those scratches on many passenger windows are frequently caused by volcanic ash.

Undercast. When you're on the ground looking up at a cloudy sky, you say it's overcast. But when a pilot is high in the sky, looking down at the clouds over Milwaukee, it's undercast. The lowest layer of clouds, hovering closest to the ground, is a **cloud deck**.

Chop and turbulence. The gentle bumps you may experience on a flight are chop (another nautical term). The flight attendant might announce: "We're entering an area of light chop." When the flight starts to resemble a roller-coaster ride, you've hit turbulence. In that case, the flight attendant might advise: "The captain is looking for some smoother air."

Bug smasher

Feet wet, feet dry. On a flight from Boston to London, the time spent over the Atlantic is the feet-wet part of the trip. Once the plane is over land again, it's feet dry.

Words At Work

Greaser. The way passengers like a pilot to touch down—so that the wheels barely graze the runway. It may feel smooth, but such a landing can eat up too much runway. Pilots actually prefer to...

Plant it. It's preferable to touch down firmly in the initial section of the runway, somewhere within the first 1,500 feet. (Major airports generally have three to six runways between 7,000 and 11,000 feet—about one and a half to two miles.) This gives pilots time for smooth, safe braking and deceleration. When the landing feels a little too firm for most pax, the pilot has planted it.

The firmness is a result of the struts on the landing gear absorbing the full rate of vertical deceleration. As with shock absorbers on a car, at a certain point you're going to feel the bump. If it's *waaaay* too firm (meaning increased levels of vertical deceleration), you risk a rubber jungle, which tends to make the pax jittery: all the oxygen masks and their attendant tubing pop out of their overhead storage. (Yes, it really happens.)

Airline Pilot

Wing walkers. The ground crew outside at your gate, ready to guide your plane to a stop. The wing walkers ensure that the two wing tips clear other planes and any surrounding vehicles. The marshallers, meanwhile, are up front, aligning the nose of the plane with the jetbridge.

Sit time. What passengers call a layover—time spent waiting in the terminal—airline staff call sit time. A layover to airline staff is a night spent in a hotel room.

Turnaround. When a pilot flies from Airport A to Airport B, picks up another load of passengers and returns to Airport A.

Glory. When you're high in the sky, with the sun behind you and a cloud deck below, every now and then there's a fleeting moment when the sun is refracted off the ice crystals in the clouds and a rainbow appears. It's not just the arc that the earthbound see, but the full, glorious circle of color around the airplane's shadow on the clouds. There just may be a silver lining to flying after all.

Weeping marshmallows, Dutching chocolate

(Cookie Baker)

Formula for a batch of
commercially-made chocolate chip cookies
Completion time: an 8-hour shift

 43,200 pounds flour

21,600 pounds sugar

10,800 pounds shortening

480 pounds salt

45 pounds vanilla

864 pounds baking soda

2,225 gallons water

21,600 pounds chocolate chips

Mix 9 tons of dough an hour. Cut into
individual pieces and bake for 12 minutes
in a 350°, 300-foot oven.
Slug and package.
Yield: 4,473,896 cookies (372,824 dozen)

Cookie Baker

A lot of dough goes into bringing a new cookie to market, as much as $25 million if it entails new baking or packaging equipment. Yet only one percent of new products destined for grocery store shelves succeeds. Here's the way most new supermarket cookies crumble:

You start off making a few small batches of a protocept— a concept cookie that begins on paper and then moves to an edible prototype. Next you scale it up, taking the concept and the batter to a pilot plant to refine the flavor and possibly the shape, too. Then you scale it up again, taking the formula, shape and flavor to a corporate (commercial) bakery. Note that professional cookie bakers use formulas, not recipes.

Hand-to-mouth. This kind of existence in cookiedom isn't so bad. It indicates a bite-size cookie, such as a two-biter. Both the marketing and packaging of cookies are geared toward how they'll be eaten.

Brown notes. Every cookie has a flavor profile, much as fragrances do, with high and low notes. A brown note is the flavor of baked caramel. A hot note might be cinnamon. And what tastes like strawberry is probably a compound of twenty different flavor chemicals. A cookie baker often licenses a compound of notes from a company that creates food-flavor profiles.

Weeping marshmallows. It's bad enough that these gooey confections have no spine. The weeping ones have no thin skin to help them congeal, either—not a good thing in cookiedom.

Enrobed cookie. One with a coating (usually chocolate).

Chocolate liquor. Nothing to do with alcohol, everything to do with whether a cookie can be described as chocolate. Take a cacao nut, roast and grind it, and it becomes a paste that hardens into baking chocolate—the chocolate liquor.

Weeping marshmallow

A cookie must be made with chocolate liquor in order to call itself chocolate. Cookies with the flavor of chocolate but no chocolate liquor have to fudge it. That's why they're called fudge, not chocolate, cookies.

Dutching. The Dutch, who have long known something about chocolate and cocoa, figured out that putting ground cocoa in an alkaline solution such as sodium bicarbonate made cocoa and chocolate liquor taste more chocolaty. You probably have some of this alkaline solution in your kitchen: it's baking soda.

Dutching the cocoa also changes the color of the cocoa and the chocolate liquor from its natural reddish hue to the browns and blacks that most of us associate with chocolate.

Shocks and seizes. When you bake cookies and cool them rapidly, you've shocked them. Small hairline cracks are often the giveaway. When you mix chocolate and water, the chocolate seizes: it gets lumpy and hard. It takes only a drop of water for this to happen, and that's the end of that chocolate—it gets tossed before it becomes cookies because the seizure cannot be reversed. This is why plant workers never wash chocolate-making equipment with water. Instead, they flush the pipes with vegetable oil.

Rework. Used as a noun rather than a verb, it's a small amount of dough left over from one batch of cookies that's put into a new batch. Most of us won't know if there's a bit of leftover dough in our cookie, but use too much rework, and both the cookie's texture and flavor could change.

Drying it down. The reason so many of us like to dip biscotti in coffee or tea is that it replenishes the moisture. Having been baked twice, biscotti have been dried down, their moisture level taken to less than three percent. This makes them shelf-stable: cookies with a long shelf life.

Slug. A dubious term for what was once a breakthrough in sanitation, the slug is the sleeve that holds certain cookies and crackers inside their boxes, thereby extending their shelf life. It is commonly a type of waxed paper or layers of paper and plastic.

There is as much psychology packed into the packaging of cookies as in the cookies themselves. In fact, the major manufacturers have psychologists on staff. If you can get your whole hand into a box to retrieve those cookies or crackers, it was planned that way. Manufacturers *want* you to be caught with your hand in the cookie box.

Dribble board. The cookies in that slug may well have undergone **penny stacking** in the bakery. They were assembled vertically, like stacks of pennies, before packaging. The dribble board is the conveyor that carries the cookies from the oven to the packaging department, where they're stacked. Depending on the cookie, along the way they might be dribbled with chocolate, as a shortbread cookie with chocolate icing is.

DWB. Definitely Will Buy. Concept cookies undergo focus group tests, which are sometimes conducted at shopping centers and referred to as **mall intercepts.** DWB consumers say they will try the product at least once.

BFD. Best Food Day. It's been around longer than a bad hair day, and

Enrobed cookie

it's the day the local paper runs the food specials. The BFD varies by region; check your local paper this coming week.

Words At Work

Slotting fees. The next time you're food shopping, see which cookies are the most visible on the store shelves and in the aisle. Manufacturers pay for that real estate through a slotting fee. The practice is not limited to cookies and grocery stores, though. Even the location of books in the superstores is driven by these promotional fees. It takes a smart cookie to know how to shop these days.

Gorillacillin

(Pharmacist)

Hippocrates, the father of modern Western medicine, prescribed food over drugs. Napoleon was leery of the "uncertain prescriptions" that collectively made up medicine. Voltaire put more faith in nature than in medicine.

They might have felt differently if they'd had a good pharmacist.

Script. Short for prescription. Rx, the familiar symbol for prescription, is an abbreviation of the Latin *recipe*, to take.

The use of Latin for writing scripts dates back centuries, to when Latin was the *lingua franca* of western Europe. Subsequently the language died, its exact meanings forever cast in stone. This provided linguistic precision for a profession that relies on exactitude. Today, the directions for taking a script still often use Latin abbreviations. How delightfully ironic that a so-called dead language helps keep people alive.

Words At Work

Sig codes. The abbreviated directions that a doctor writes on the script for how the patient should take the medication. *Sig* is short for the Latin *signa* or *signetur,* meaning "let it be labeled."

Some common sig codes that a doctor scrawls on a script:

a.c.	*ante cibum*	before meals
b.i.d.	*bis in die*	twice a day
h.s.	*hora somni*	at bedtime
p.o.	*per os*	by mouth
q.d.	*quaque die*	daily
q.h.	*quaque hora*	every hour
q.i.d.	*quater in die*	four times a day

DAW. An English abbreviation that stands for Dispense As Written. Doctors write this when prescribing a specific brand name of a drug. It means that a generic substitute is not acceptable. ❋

Formulary. The list of drugs that an insurance company allows or that a hospital prefers.

Working with riddles. What pharmacists say when

trying to work with (or around) insurance companies.

NDC. National Drug Code. Every prescribed and OTC (over-the-counter) medication has such an identification number, and it is always printed on the packaging.

OBECALP. It looks like a series of random letters...until you reverse them. If this is on your script, your doctor has just prescribed a P-L-A-C-E-B-O for you.

Covering the patient. "We're covering the patient for pseudomonas," a hospital pharmacist might say, meaning that they're protecting the patient with a drug (in this case, an antibiotic) that has activity against, or fights, that particular organism.

Gorillacillin. A broad-spectrum antibiotic that has activity against many organisms.

Bugs & drugs. Organisms and antibiotics. Doctors need to know which drugs kill which bugs so that they can prescribe the proper antibiotic, antiviral or antifungal agent for a specific illness.

Practicing polypharmacy. When pharmacists remark that "Doctor So-and-So practices polypharmacy," they're indicating their disapproval of a doctor who, in their opinion, has prescribed too many medications for a patient.

Duplicate therapy. A close cousin to the above. Let's say that on Monday the pharmacist fills a script for 800 mg of Motrin for a patient. On Wednesday, that same patient has a script for Naprosyn. Both are nonsteroidal anti-inflammatory drugs, or NSAIDs. The patient needs one or the other, but not both. Pharmacists alert prescribers to such duplications.

Double counter. A patient who counts the pills in a bottle even though the pharmacist already has. And even when it's a manufacturer's bottle.

Vitamin R. The nickname for Ritalin, the oft-prescribed drug for attention-deficit disorder.

Vitamin V. Also known as Big Blue. If you guessed it's the code name for Viagra, you're right.

Vitamin V

Brompton's Cocktail. Another code name that most likely comes via the Royal Brompton Hospital in London. This one is for a medicinal cocaine mix that helps some cancer patients manage their pain.

Pharmacist

Pharmacists categorize controlled substances (also known as scheduled medications) such as cocaine by a numbering system, using the Roman numerals I, II, III, IV and V. The lower the number, the stronger and more addictive the substance.

Medicinal cocaine and marijuana are classified CI. (The C stands for controlled.) Pharmacists are usually allowed to dispense them only in a hospital, adhering to strict guidelines. They must keep CII prescription medications, such as a pain pill that you could get hooked on, in a locked cabinet for which only they have the key—in the narcotic room in a hospital, or a narcotic safe in a retail pharmacy. If a CII script isn't filled within seven days of being written, it's null and void.

Certain other pain relievers are CIII medications, certain tranquilizers are CIV, and some strong cough syrups are CV.

Compounding. Not that long ago, pharmacists had to compound, or mix, many prescriptions according to certain formulas. It was roughly the equivalent of cooking from scratch because no packaged meal was available. Today that's changed; most scripts come packaged in a tablet, capsule, liquid or tube. But some scripts still are made from scratch.

A dermatologist, for example, might prescribe a mixture of hydroquinone powder and isopropyl alcohol to be prepared as a suspension for treating acne. (In a suspension, the compounds dissolve but not completely. You need to shake before using, much as you would an oil and vinegar salad dressing.)

A few pharmacies are reviving the practice of compounding, creating what they call personalized medicine. It ranges from hormones to vitamin mixtures to topical pain remedies that are made from scratch so that they're customized to each patient's needs. Some expressions you could hear in a compounding pharmacy:

"Run it through the mill." You might feel that you've been through the mill after you pay for some of your scripts, but in a compounding pharmacy, chances are your script really has been. The pharmacist literally runs the ingredients for a cream or an ointment through a mill. Big chunks of powders are placed between two rollers, which mash them into smaller particles. This helps to mix all the ingredients thoroughly and smoothes the powders to a creamy consistency.

Pharmacist

"You need to color it up." Another technique for thoroughly mixing powders before they're dispensed into capsules. Pharmacists may add pharmaceutical-grade food coloring as a visual gauge. You color up the compound to make the color consistent throughout the powder. This indicates that it's evenly mixed.

"Time to torch it." It sounds incendiary, but it's just a signal to the staff that the tubing or other packaging is ready to be heat-sealed. Then it's on to the next made-to-order medicine.

❋ Footnote to DAW:

Drugs have two names, generic and brand, plus a chemical formula. The brand name Tylenol, for example, is known generically as acetaminophen. Generic names, which by law must appear on the label, sometimes use cues to indicate the type of drug they are. For example, certain drugs used to lower cholesterol end in "statin."

If you've ever noticed that drug names sound different from one another, this is also regulated by law. No one brand name can sound too much like another, to prevent potential mix-ups.

"EQ the VO with the SFX"

(Television Promo Producer)

"A live report at eleven." Chances are you've seen them flash across your TV screen and, the networks and stations hope, paid attention to them. They are the short promotional spots, usually thirty seconds but perhaps only four, exhorting you to stay up for the news, settle in for the movie, tune in to the final episode, catch the late-breaking announcement and otherwise pay attention to what's rolling across your screen. *Just please oh please don't touch that remote.*

The creators of these promos marshal words, graphics, music, sound effects and video footage to try to keep you watching. The producer decides what the message is, writes it, then adds the video to support it. The editor splices the video and audio together. Both work to the overall tone that the creative director sets as to how the spot should look and sound.

Television Promo Producer

Talent. The people you see on camera. The talent could be a news anchor, a reporter or an actor. In a news promo, for example, the producer might decide that the anchor should be the main talent in the spot.

Thirty. A thirty-second spot. Typed, it appears as :30. The producer first asks the creative director, "What length do you want?" The director replies, "This is a thirty."

Bites. The rest of us call them sound bites, but those who use them say, "I've got three really good bites for this spot." Bites are the memorable, provocative or funny short phrases that the people being interviewed or the characters in the show say. They add punch to a spot.

If the producer has written too much narrative, or copy, the creative director might say, "Your thirty looks a little copy-heavy. Can you cut the copy and use more bites?"

Stand-up. The script of the talent on the scene, often recorded specifically for the promo. The talent addresses the audience directly (and almost always standing up). A producer might say, "I need a stand-up from the reporter in front of the courthouse. I'll use VO for the rest of the spot."

VO. The voiceover, or VO, belongs to an announcer who's heard but not seen. Say V-O and you'll sound like a pro.

B-roll. Nothing to do with the ratings of movies. It's footage, sometimes stock shots, that supports the announcement beyond the bites and stand-ups. A spot on rising medical costs, for example, could include B-roll of a hospital emergency room entrance.

The term dates back to the days when TV news producers used film to capture footage. Because of both time and technological constraints, they kept all interview elements on one reel—the audio, or A-roll—and the other supporting footage on a separate reel, the B-roll.

Takes. The announcer's or talent's reading from a script. It often takes several takes to get the best read, or delivery, of each line. Cautious producers do a safety, an extra take, to make sure there's a good read.

EQ. Equalizing the audio, whether it's a voice or an SFX (sound effect). When the music is dominating the VO, the producer says, "Let's EQ the VO to make it pop."

Television Promo Producer

Scratch track. "I've got to get my VO tracked," the producer says, meaning, "I've got to have my voiceover recorded." But before the real thing happens, producers might do a recording themselves, in an edit session, to align the video with the audio. This preliminary recording is the scratch track.

Screeners and dailies. Promo spots for movies and television programs start in one of two ways. They may be created from raw footage, called dailies, or from fully edited programs, called screeners. When the production company that owns the movie sends it to the station, the producer has a screener to work from. Most producers use screeners if they're available but have dailies to fall back on.

Overlaid on the bottom of the screen of this video is a time code that measures the video in intervals of one-thirtieth of a second (a frame—more on that coming up). These give producers signposts that tell them where to pull a bite or a clip. Let's say the screener is two hours, twenty minutes and eight seconds long. Partway through is a bite the producer wants. The time code shows the producer that the bite occurs at 1: 10: 04: 28, or one hour, ten minutes, four seconds and the twenty-eighth frame in that second.

Post and mix. This is where the fun begins: the producer and editor meet in the editing studio to pull together, or post, the final spot. After that, the producer might work with an audio engineer to EQ music and VO and add SFX, elements collectively known as the mix. A producer might estimate that "I need a day and a half to post and another morning for the mix."

Frames. In every second of video, there are thirty frames. Frames give the producer a point of reference when deciding on the visual transitions in a spot. (Before video, back in the days of film, you could actually see these frames.) Some of those transitions might be cuts, dissolves or white flashes.

Dissolve. Whereas a cut is a standard transition between video clips, a dissolve is softer and slower, taking its time in superimposing one image on the other. "Let's do a three-frame dissolve," the producer says.

White flash. The opposite of a dissolve. This transition

technique is used to create faster-paced spots. White flashes happen in about four frames. One way to create a white flash would be: two frames for the dissolve to white, one frame of all white, then the new video. The "live, late-breaking news" announcements often use this technique for added drama. It's so fast, you don't really see the flash.

Tag. The message, usually at the end of the spot but sometimes at both the end and the beginning, reminding you where and when to tune in—"tonight at eleven, only on Action News." The producer could decide that "I want the anchor for talent but the announcer can do the tag."

Fade to black. Yes, they really use this term to signify the end. In reality, it's several frames of black that appear on the screen, but the viewer's eye sees it simply as a fade to black.

Words At Work

Sample Promo Script

:30 Action News At 11

VIDEO	AUDIO
11pm Action News full-screen graphic	(:03 top tag) VO: Tonight at 11 on Action News...
Generic B-roll of kids in classroom	ANCHOR: Is your child's school making the grade? We'll bring you the latest test results and why one
Principal Jones shot	principal says the scores are all wrong.
Jim Smith stand-up	STAND-UP: This garbage dump is loaded with trash that should have gone to the recycling center. I'm Jim Smith and I'll have a live report to tell you who is responsible.
B-roll from helicopter of city hall, close-up of crack in outer wall, wide shot of workers evacuating building	ANCHOR: Plus, new details on the sinkhole that's threatening to swallow city hall. Find out if downtown will be shut down for another day.
On-camera bite from city hall worker	BITE (city hall worker): "It's just not safe to be in that building."
11pm Action News full-screen end graphic	(:05 end tag) VO: Tonight at 11 on Action News. All local. All the time.

Wooing SMERFs, crunching REVPAR

(Hotelier)

When you book a hotel room, you can either pay the rack rate or negotiate. But first, be sure to bone up on shoulders, know if you can swing a comp and understand the value of being in a SMERF group. When all else fails, as one hotel professional advises, "Look at the parking lot. If it's empty, negotiate."

Racks and shoulders. The rack rate is the advertised rate, so called because those are the rates printed in the rack cards, or promotional materials. You have a better chance of negotiating off-the-rack rates during the off-season or even the shoulder season. Shoulders are the months leading into and out of peak season.

Comp. A free stay, compliments of the hotel. For the hotel, it's an incentive for tour guides and meeting planners. They in turn use it as a negotiating tool—one comp room for every twenty-five booked, for example, to accommodate the meeting staff, guest speakers and so on.

Fam tours. Also called fam trips, these are special days the hotel devotes to tour guides, meeting planners, visitor and convention bureau personnel and the like to familiarize them with its various amenities and services. Expect to be comped.

SMERF. Social, Military, Educational, Religious and Fraternal associations. All five groups are desirable markets for conference hotels, especially during the off-season and shoulder season.

Precon. "Let's schedule a precon for Monday," the hotel's convention planner says, meaning, let's have a preconference meeting with the client. It's usually held the day before a conference or convention begins.

REVPAR. Revenue per available room. REVPAR tells a hotel what a room is worth during a particular month or season. In peak season, a room is worth more than in the shoulder season. The front desk uses REVPAR when negotiating rates. ※

City ledger. If a hotel is billing an account directly rather than on a credit card, the business office posts the amount to its city ledger and from there bills the client. Banquet costs are often posted to a city ledger. Companies that frequently send their clients and out-of-town staff to a specific hotel may have a city ledger account.

Transresidential. A long word for someone staying a long time in a hotel, to the point of moving in. Think of *The Man Who Came to Dinner*, but with his checkbook. It's a behind-the-desk term, though. "Permanent guests" is how the hotel staff publicly refers to these live-ins. In most states, when transresidentials decide to move in for more than thirty days, their stay is considered a lease.

Sleep-out. What some might consider the ideal guest: one who pays but doesn't stay.

Let's say you're visiting Los Angeles for two weeks and want to spend a night in Las Vegas. Rather than packing up two weeks' worth of luggage, you simply pay your hotel in Los Angeles for the full two weeks and leave most of your luggage there during your overnight in Vegas.

Words At Work

Sleeper. "We've got a sleeper in 201." Such an announcement is likely to send the front desk scrambling. It has nothing to do with the door handle that still displays the Do Not Disturb message at noon. A sleeper is the guest nobody knew about until Housekeeping discovered that the room was occupied. Or the guest who booked for two nights and stayed for three.

Walk. The flip side of the sleeper. There you are, with your room reservation guarantee, and there's the hotel, with no room for you. In which case, the staff walks you to another hotel that's agreed to take you in. Expect to be comped.

❋ Here's an example of how REVPAR is calculated:
A hotel estimates a month's revenue based on historical data—e.g., how much has the establishment taken in for June during the past several years? Assume that a 100-room hotel budgets $250,000 in revenue for June. The REVPAR numbers would crunch like this:

$$\$250,000 \div (100 \text{ rooms} \times 30 \text{ days}) =$$
$$\$250,000 \div 3,000 =$$
$$\$83.33 \text{ REVPAR}$$

This is the minimum the hotel needs to charge for each room to meet its revenue plan.

Hickeys, halos and hot spots

(Printer)

Never mind helping a fledgling country win its independence and that business with the kite. More than anything else, Benjamin Franklin wanted to be remembered as a printer. His epitaph reads:

> The Body of
> B. Franklin,
> Printer;
> Like the Cover of an old Book,
> Its contents torn out,
> And stript of its Lettering and Gilding,
> Lies here, Food for Worms,
> But the Work shall not be wholly lost:
> For it will, as he believ'd, appear once more,
> In a new & more perfect Edition,
> Corrected and amended
> By the Author.

Those author's emendations and corrections are technically known as AAs, for author's alterations. They are the eleventh-hour changes that an author or graphic designer makes to a piece that everybody thought was ready to go on press, meaning ready to be printed. Franklin, ever frugal, probably would have reconsidered such revisions: printers charge for those AAs.

Dummy. Smart designers prepare a dummy, or preliminary layout, of a print piece for the client. It's far less costly to do another dummy than to have to reprint a finished piece (and may prevent some of those AAs). Often the actual images are not yet available at dummy stage. A designer inserts another, comparable image into the dummy and marks it FPO—For Position Only.

Gang up. Though it sounds like something frantic clients do to printers when they're on deadline, it's actually what printers do to save the client money: they gang two or more similar print jobs on the same press run. "Let's gang these four jobs," a printer will say—because in doing so, it makes the most efficient use of the paper and print setup.

Printer

Halo. When an image on the page is unintentionally blurred because the dot pattern is not registering correctly on the paper, the pattern that emerges resembles a halo. It's just one of the many ways that printing can bedevil printers.

Printer's devil. Back in Franklin's era, the printer's devil was the pressman's apprentice, helping him with the inky, messy work. One theory for the term is the propensity for the pressman to refer to such a young lad as "that devil of a boy." Mark Twain was a printer's devil in his youth.

Hickeys and hot spots. These get printers hot under the collar. They're specks of dirt that get embedded in the paper, or a rip in the film or plate that leaves a blank spot on the page.

Butt fit. Something else printers get worked up about, and this time happily so. It means that various ink colors came together without crossing into each other's territory. Considering the numerous perils that can befall ink, it's a wonder any of it fits. Ink can also stick, cake, plug, mottle, scuff, streak, scum or create an odd pattern effect known as moiré.

Words At Work

Blanket. On the printing press, in between the plate with the ink and the paper that it's going on is a rubber-coated pad that acts as the go-between, transferring the ink to the paper. The go-between is the blanket, and this kind of printing is called offset or lithography. Blankets can get wrinkled, torn and dirty, causing those hickeys.

Gutter. The inner margin where two facing pages come together in a book, catalog or brochure. Printers don't want type to fall into the gutter; they'll be in a similar place with their client if it does.

Dummy with an FPO

Widows and orphans. Short lines of type at the top and bottom of pages. One lonely word left to fend all by itself on a line is also usually referred to as a widow. Widows and orphans drive designers and proofreaders nuts; most readers don't even notice. Fortunately there are no missing children to contend with. There is, however, ghosting.

Printer

Ghosting. Depending on whether it was intentional, ghosting can be good or bad. Sometimes printers and designers want you to see a faint image, one that's been ghosted back. It's when that ghost comes unbidden that a problem arises, as when wet ink from one press sheet migrates to another stacked on top of it, or the errant ink on a dirty plate ends up on a press sheet.

Four over one. Four colors on one side of the paper and one color on the other. These magical four are usually process colors: cyan (blue), magenta, yellow and key, which is black.

Printers and designers often refer to these four colors as CMYK. In a four-color run, the printer must place the colors on top of one another with great care. Black has shades of every color, so it provides the guide, or key, to the placement of one color on the other—hence the K.

Virtually any color can be created or simulated with varying combinations and densities of this gang of four.

Trap. When it comes to ink, a trap is a good thing. It

indicates how well the ink colors lie on the paper during the printing process. Colors are applied sequentially, within tenths of a second of each other. The most common sequence is the C-M-Y-K. If the inks aren't lying on the paper correctly, the press person will say, "It's not trapping well."

Saddle stitch. One way to bind a book, magazine or catalog. The result looks like staples but it's actually a wire that's stitched in by machine. In order to stitch the printed piece, you have to straddle it on the bindery machinery the way you would a saddle over the back of a horse. After a certain thickness (usually sixty pages), saddle stitching won't work, so printers glue the pages instead. This is known as perfect bound, which is how this book was bound.

Signature. The name given to a printed sheet after it has been folded for binding. In traditional binding, signatures are in increments divisible by four.

Signature has its roots in the Latin signum, mark or sign. In Ben Franklin's time and earlier, the printer placed a mark in the lower margin of successive sheets, or leaves, of the pages to indicate the proper sequence for binding. When the sheets were folded and gathered (some printers still call folds and gathers F&Gs), identical marks signaled that it was a signature.

Catchword. This is a word you might even catch some printers on because catchwords are no longer needed. But in Ben Franklin's day the catchword, like the signum, provided a visual cue to the binder as to the correct sequence of the pages. At the bottom of a page, printers included the first word that appeared on the next: the catchword.

The custom predates Franklin and even Gutenberg. The owners of books would often use the catchword as doodling terrain, drawing pictures around it. In a time when book pages were not numbered, they proved to be quite helpful when looking for a particular place in a book.

Catchword and *catch phrase* still live on in print, even though the practice has been abandoned. Today we use the terms to mean something said so often, it's like a slogan. "Publish or perish" is one. Printers might well agree.

Blowing for dollars

[Symphony Orchestra Musician]

An orchestra adheres to its own form of government.
Where else in America does one person with a baton call all
the shots? And it's one of the few instances where those with
the quietest voices get front-row seats: the string section is
almost always in front, to either side of the conductor's
podium. In the center is the woodwind section (flutes,
piccolo, clarinets, bass clarinet, oboes, English horn,
bassoons and contrabassoon). In the back and fanning out
slightly is the brass section (trumpets, trombones, French
horns and tuba). The percussionists (drums, cymbals,
timpani, gongs and triangles) are the farthest back, along
with the piano and harp.

An orchestra assembles seventy-five to one hundred and
twenty personalities into a space that is usually no larger
than seventy feet wide and forty-nine feet deep, with the goal

of making beautiful music together. That's despite the strings often accusing the brass of playing too loudly, and the woodwinds sometimes chiming in. As for the one wielding the baton—the truth is, not every musician watches the conductor all of the time.

Stick picker. If you guessed that this is the name the orchestra members irreverently confer on the wand wagger (oops! make that the conductor), you're correct. But the musicians themselves and their instruments are not exempt from playful sobriquets:

wire choir	the string section
bones or slush pumpers	trombones
brassholes	members of the brass section
rain catcher	tuba
licorice sticks	clarinets

Service. An umbrella term for either a rehearsal or a concert. A musician might say, "We've got a service tomorrow afternoon and one tomorrow night," meaning that there's a rehearsal or concert that afternoon and another that evening.

Words At Work

"We have a double rehearsal today." Back-to-back services, with just a break in between.

"She's doubling." Sometimes a musician plays two different instruments during a service. A violinist might also play the mandolin, for example. Doubling usually means more pay.

"He's got chops." Said admiringly of another musician who plays well. The compliment is a coveted one, as it speaks to technique, range and endurance. It also stands for the sum of a musician's most important anatomical parts: fingers and, for brass and woodwind, lips and tongue. After a double rehearsal, the musician who plays the rain catcher might say, "Boy, my chops are tired."

Footballs. Whole notes, which are held longer than quarter and eighth notes. (And you thought musicians never talked sports.)

"The page was black." The musical score was dense with notes, commanding superior technique.

Clams. Code word for mistakes. Even the best musicians

occasionally hit the wrong notes. If one announces, "That was a real clambake," you know it hasn't been the best of days for making music.

Foot shuffle. Applause, orchestra style. Next time you go to the symphony, watch the players' feet. The musicians often shuffle their feet in appreciation of a player who's just nailed a solo or an especially difficult passage.

Run-out. A performance away from the orchestra's home base. It differs from a concert tour, which features a number of different venues. The Chicago Symphony Orchestra, for example, usually performs at Symphony Center in Chicago.

Wand wagger

Occasionally, though, the orchestra performs a run-out in Ann Arbor, Michigan, or Madison, Wisconsin.

Fly-out. A run-out that you fly back from right after the performance.

Blowing for dollars. A brass player's audition.

Blind audition. Aspiring orchestra musicians audition anonymously. They are heard but literally not seen, so that the audition panel judges them on merit without being swayed by gender, race, looks or even name. The players perform behind a screen and are referred to by a number only.

Foot shuffle

Even the walkway that a player uses to get onstage is carpeted, so that the *click-click* of high heels doesn't give a woman away. (Read *Blink* by Malcolm Gladwell for some fascinating stories on how blind auditions changed the face of orchestras.)

"Today's squeak is tomorrow's audition." A novel way to talk about setting a new benchmark. What may be a difficult high note to hit this year in a new piece could end up being a test piece at auditions a few years from now. Until such time, you might hear this:

"That's a note an octave above my salary." A note that's difficult to reach.

Pushing the tempo. Playing faster than you're supposed to so that you get ahead of the beat (and everybody else). Also known as having an edge on the tempo.

Symphony Orchestra Musician

Shedding the part. Practicing the music. *Shedding* is a shortened version of woodshed—originally, the name musicians gave to a quiet place removed from the fray where they could go off and practice in peace. "You need to woodshed that," meaning, "You need to practice some more," is another variation.

"Start at the northwest corner." What a conductor says to the musicians, meaning: start at the beginning of the piece. And, the conductor might add, watch my wand.

Angels, orphans, zombies, vultures

(Venture Capitalist)

Somewhere between "hope springs eternal" and "fools rush in" lies the kingdom of venture capital. One definition of a venture capitalist, or VC, is a professional optimist who's allowed to use other people's money, along with the VC's own, to fund what seems like a great idea. The odds of its being so are not great. On average, only about twenty percent of funded ventures really take off, while approximately forty percent simply tank. Darwinism rules.

Depending on whether you see the world through rose-colored glasses or with a jaundiced eye, you may view venture capitalism as the ultimate validation of the entrepreneurial spirit or a place where angels (wisely) fear to tread.

Angel. Sometimes before a venture capitalist group appears on the scene, individual investors give a start-up its first financial wings. The sum is relatively modest by VC standards, although the hope is for a fast return that is anything but that. Angels often take the form of family members or friends. Occasionally they are wealthy investors who like playing long shots.

Orphan. A start-up venture with no VC.

Elevator pitch. Savvy orphans sharpen their pitch to a VC so that it takes no longer than an elevator ride to the fourteenth floor to deliver it.

Elevator pitch

Alpha. Referring to ventures as start-ups may be a bit optimistic. Often these companies are merely think-ups: not only do they lack revenue, but they often don't have their product or service ready to sell. So there's a testing phase before it can be brought to market. The first round of tests, the alpha, reveals the changes that need to be made to make the product or service successful.

Beta. Products or services that are almost ready for market and are tested by a few key customers. Often they need more fine-tuning if they are to be truly marketable. The tip-off for the investors is when the start-up says, "The product is virtually ready for market." (Another common delusion on the start-up's part: "The management team is in place and fully qualified.")

Crowded space. Too many companies vying for the same market niche. Venture capitalists usually steer clear of a company that's in a crowded space because it's that much harder to pick a winner.

Barriers to entry. Various ways that start-ups encounter the NO ADMITTANCE signs in their industry. Technical superiority on the part of existing businesses can be a barrier to entry, as can a highly efficient distribution system or a killer network of strategic partnerships. Breaking through these barriers is one of the costs of admission into business. Raising these barriers once you're in is a way to keep more competition out, and to add value to your company.

Ten-bagger

Vintage year. The first year

that a venture capital partnership invests. Like wine, some vintages are better than others. While 1996 was a very good year, let's not talk about 1999. Also, please don't mention "Internet" and "bubble" in the same breath, and don't bring up tulips again. ✽

Hockey stick. Revenue growth that has been flat but then spikes dramatically and grows exponentially. On a graph, the growth rate resembles a hockey stick: flat across until it hits that inflection point and shoots up. At least, this is how the entrepreneur forecasts it. The reality more often resembles the movement of a bouncing ball: up and down, up and down.

Ten-bagger. An investment whose rate of return is ten times the original sum invested.

Other people's money (OPM). Venture capitalists rarely go it alone. They act as the general partner for a pool of investors that are the limited partners—the other people.

Mezzanine. A level of financing that helps in capitalizing a company along the way to IPO status. IPO stands for Initial Public Offering, a start-up's first publicly traded shares of stock. It also represents one exit strategy for venture capitalists. Even though venture capitalists generally don't pull out all of their money at the IPO, as one investment banker puts it, "Now you've brought in the unsuspecting public."

Liquidity event. An IPO is one such. A VC prays to the cash gods for a liquidity event, as it's the green light to turn ownership in the start-up into greenbacks. Merging with a publicly traded company or selling the start-up are other ways to get cash out of the deal.

Zombie. A company that lives and breathes and that's about it. There's no financial growth and no liquidity for the shareholders. Zombies, not surprisingly, are not a favorite among the VC set.

Roach motel. A company whose liquidity potential has dried up. Picture the self-contained traps you can buy at the hardware store to catch creepy-crawlies. In similar fashion, a VC firm took the bait and put its money into the venture— now the money's stuck there.

Piggyback and drag-along. Venture capitalists establish specific rights when they invest, creating different classes of stock and spelling out certain rights in the shareholder agreement. For instance, venture capitalists almost always hold preferred stock, rather than common stock—the investment equivalent of flying first class rather than coach. (The golden rule: those that have the gold, rule.)

Piggyback and drag-along are two other rights. Piggyback rights ensure that the VC's shares are part of the initial stock offering, when prices are sometimes the rosiest. Drag-along rights allow a VC to drag the rest of the investors along in a decision, such as to sell the company.

Green shoe. A clause in the IPO that has investment bankers (the underwriters) clicking their heels in glee. It means the newly minted public company can sell a few more shares than originally planned (with the underwriters' blessing) because the stock is hot. It's named after the

Burn rate

company that first thought to do this: the Green Shoe Company. For some investment bankers, exercising a green shoe clause may be the best workout they get—they walk away with more green in their pockets.

Words At Work

Burn rate. The amount of money a business spends each month. If the company spends more than its cash on hand, the burn rate can trigger a cram-down.

Cram-down. What happens when a start-up stumbles rather than falls, and new investors add money, or the original investors add more money. Either way, it results in the founding partners' equity going down, sometimes significantly so.

Founderitis. A malady that sets in when a founder can't let go of his or her brainchild, even though professional management has stepped in.

Vulture capitalists. When a new company struggles with too much debt and too little cash, it leaves itself open to a predatory investor swooping down like a vulture and scooping it up for a bargain-basement price. On the other hand, it might be better to be carried away by a vulture than to be left as potential roadkill.

Flameout. When a start-up burns through all the available cash and there is no vulture ex machina, hope is extinguished, and operations cease. But the fiery image is

Venture Capitalist

fitting. Remember that the phoenix, ever the optimist, always rises from its ashes.

✸ Footnote to vintage year:

When too many investors put more money into a commodity or concept than it's worth, a bubble forms and then rises, ineluctably, to its occasion: it bursts.

Fancy a tulip bulb's being worth more than three-quarters of a million dollars in today's money—and this in the 1600s. That's how extreme it was in Europe during the great tulip speculation. Dutch merchants created an artificial demand for the flower, which had been introduced from Turkey and had, by virtue of a virus that infected it, produced variations in color. (Later, growers realized that they could create these colors by conventional breeding methods.) The government finally stepped in to quell the frenzy, prompting the merchants to unload their stockpiles of bulbs and causing the market—along with the whole Dutch economy—to collapse. The bloom was definitely off.

Today tulip, in VC-speak, is a code word for an overheated and unrealistic market that's soon to burst.

White goods that aren't

(Waste Manager)

The joke in garbage circles is that "everybody wants us to pick it up, nobody wants us to put it down." Just what is it that they're picking up? Garbage? Trash? Rubbish? To those of us doing the pitching, it may not matter what this flotsam and jetsam are called. But for those who pick it up (and put it down), different discards constitute discrete types of waste.

Garbage. A lot of the stuff you throw away is, in fact, garbage. Generally speaking, it's anything in the kitchen that ends up in the wastebasket. If it's animal or vegetable, it also earns the unsavory technical description of putrescible (pronounced "pew-TRESS-uh-bull," or *eeuww*). The pastrami that's lived a long life in your refrigerator will end its life as garbage if you don't eat it soon. But when your refrigerator has lived more than a good life, it's not garbage.

Waste Manager

(Correct terminology coming up.) The junk mail that you toss along with that pastrami, however, *is* garbage.

Trash. Something of an umbrella term, trash includes yard wastes, such as hedge trimmings, and also bulky wastes, such as that old recliner that's now in decline.

Rubbish. "What a load of rubbish!" Technically, that's true only if you're referring to wood-based wastes such as big stacks of paper. Nineteenth-century lexicographers called it *rubbrish* or *rubbage.*

White good. We may call it an appliance, but when that stove or fridge is destined for the trash heap, it's a white good. Never mind that it might be avocado or stainless steel—back in the 1940s and 50s, almost all appliances were white, and the name stuck.

Landfill. If you want to get a waste professional's dander up, refer to that lined, covered, vented and monitored mound o' waste, which costs a bundle to operate and even more to close, as a dump instead of a landfill. The truth about trash (and garbage and rubbish): because of environmental regulations, it costs a lot more to put it down than it does to pick it up. Just the cost of acquiring the environmental permits to run a landfill makes it all but impossible to be a mom-and-pop operation. It's easily hundreds of thousands of dollars.

Garbage juice. The technical term for the rain and liquids that trickle down inside the landfill is leachate. In other words: garbage juice. In other words: *eeuww.* Garbage juice is either contained within the landfill or pumped into a sewage treatment plant.

Tipping fee. Don't try this kind of tipping at a restaurant. The tipping fee is what it costs to get a load of waste off the truck—to tip it off the truck bed—and into the landfill. It's usually measured on a per-ton basis or, if there's no scale at the facility, per volume or cubic yard.

Roll-off

Roll-off. Nothing to do with water and a duck's back. Rather, it's the large container that can be disengaged from the back of a garbage truck and plopped in the front yard during major home renovations. Much of what goes into a roll-off, besides the neighbors' ire, is C&D, or construction and demolition, debris. Some businesses, such as grocery stores, have enclosed roll-offs that get hooked up to compactors.

Packers and clams. The different trucks that do the picking up. Packer trucks are the ones that wake you up at 5:00 a.m. on garbage days. Clam trucks, with their large extending arms, do yard wastes and white goods.

Red-bag waste. Biomedical waste, also known as biohazardous waste. It's often collected at its source (such as hospitals and doctors' offices) in red plastic bags. A few years ago, a high-end department store caused a kerfuffle among waste professionals when it sold decorative garbage bags with its name emblazoned on them. Why the fuss? The bags were bright red, and the concern was that they would be mistaken for red-bag waste.

Special wastes. What makes them special is that they're so darn hard to get rid of. Old tires and dead batteries are among the wastes that require special handling.

Waste stream. Banish all images of rivers of garbage

floating by. This is how industry professionals refer to garbage, trash, rubbish, white goods and special wastes *in toto.*

Single-stream recycling. If you really want to impress your trash-minded friends, drop this term into the conversation. In this scenario, all residentially generated papers—junk mail, newspapers, magazines, cardboard boxes—are mixed in with bottles and cans for recycling pickups.

Murf. The phonetic pronunciation of MRF, or materials recovery facility. That's the clunky name given to the recycling plant that sorts the various papers, cans and bottles.

Incidental to the load. Material in a load of waste that's present in a negligible amount, sometimes described as *de minimis.* A half-filled bottle of nail polish remover in a truckload of other household pickups, for example, is considered incidental

Special wastes

to the load—even though larger quantities of commercially generated nail polish remover are classified as hazardous waste when discarded.

Waste Manager

Chain of custody. The equivalent of the paper trail in documenting the origin, transport and disposal of hazardous wastes. The originators have to document these wastes. The disposal sites have to document that they accepted them and where they put them. This is one stack of papers that is not destined for the rubbish heap.

Dummy juice and cereal boxes

(Perfume Maker)

"To trade in perfume is to belong to romance," trilled an English man of letters in the 1920s. To the customer at the fragrance counter, it's a beautifully packaged bottle of *parfum* with an evocative scent. For those who bring it to market, it's the final step in a production process that involves freelance noses, hollowed-out hockey pucks and bottles filled with dummy juice. So much for romance.

"Who's your nose?" Most people know a fragrance by brand name, but the company that owns the brand depends on its fragrance house to formulate the oils. One person, or nose, in the fragrance house develops a scent. If no one is available in-house, the company hires a freelance nose.

Tooling the bottles up. Creating the design and mold for the perfume bottle. A commonly heard sentiment: "We need to tool up by this date in order to make launch."

Perfume Maker

Third-party fillers. The company contracts with third-party fillers, also called co-packers, to produce and fill the glass perfume bottles to the company's specifications.

Pucks. Plastic holders that keep the bottles upright on the production line. They resemble hollowed-out hockey pucks.

Actuator. The small cap on the top of a pump that sprays a fragrance out of its bottle. On the production line, the actuator and pump are either crimped on with a metal collar or screwed on. For most fragrances, the pump and actuator have replaced the atomizer, which resembled a small rubber ball that you squeezed.

In-line labeling. Affixing a label to the package or bottle while it's on the production line. The most common for bottles is the base label, the unobtrusive and frequently transparent sticker that you probably don't even notice on the bottom of the bottle. It usually indicates the net weight, manufacturer and batch code, which is unique to each production run and tells the manufacturer where and when production took place.

Off-line customization. The same bottle of perfume is packaged and labeled differently for different stores. Manufacturers keep the packaging generic until sales forecasts come in with estimated counts for the various customization options. One account may want an anti-theft label only, another may want this plus a scratch-and-sniff label.

An anti-theft label is common for mass-market stores because they have no salespeople to hand customers the product and keep watch for light fingers. These bottles are apt to come encased in that tough, clear plastic called a clamshell, with the anti-theft label attached to the carton. Usually a plain white adhesive-backed label, it's sensitized so that if the package bypasses checkout, where it's deactivated, the alarm goes off.

Prestige channel. High-end department stores are one of the many sales outlets, or channels, for perfume. They constitute the prestige channel. Next in the hierarchy are mid-tier stores, then mass-market and club stores. On the bottom rung are wholesalers, who sell discontinued products

Perfume Maker

to a liquidator. A new fragrance usually launches in the prestige stores. Its success determines how long management sells it only at the prestige level before rolling it out to the mid-tiers or mass channels.

Cereal box. The promotional blitz, or launch, of a new fragrance includes lots of print pieces, known collectively as collateral. The next time a new fragrance launches, check the prestige stores to see if their displays contain large boxes with pictures of the product or related imagery (shots of its celebrity spokesperson, for example). This collateral is the cereal box. It's an empty, oversized box, as wide as 22 inches and as high as 27½ inches, that has the plain contours of a box of Cheerios but looks a whole lot sexier, thanks to the lavishly produced images.

Dummy juice in a factice

Dummy juice. Ever wonder if it's really perfume in the huge bottle the prestige stores display? It's not, but it isn't just colored water, either. Alcohol and preservatives are part of the mix and ensure that this dummy juice looks smart for weeks. Once the color is right, the brew is exposed to variations in temperature and light to make sure it's stable.

Factice. An oversized version of the fragrance's actual bottle, the factice is the display piece that holds the dummy juice. The French, whose word it is, say "foc-TEESS." Miniature bottles, called replicas, are also often part of a launch. These contain the real juice, and the bottles are about a quarter to a third the size of the standard bottles being sold (usually 1.7 or 3.3 ounces in the United States). Both factices and replicas have become collectibles.

On-pack. A variation of buy-one-get-one. A replica might be included with a regular size bottle of fragrance, and it will literally be attached to the packaging. Think of this on-pack as the sidecar on a motorcycle.

"Is that in our stable?" Is that one of our company's products?

"Are we getting the sell-through?" A manufacturer sells to stores. But that's only half the selling story. The transaction is complete only when the product sells through to the stores' customers. The better the sell-through, the fewer the returns from the stores, and the happier the manufacturer.

OOS and POOS. Both rhyme with *lose*, as in losing the sale because you're either out of stock (OOS) or potentially out of stock (POOS).

Flanker. After the successful launch of a fragrance, a company might say, "Let's revisit this in six months to see if there's a chance of doing a flanker." Also known as a variant, it's another version of the same fragrance—a lighter version of a heavy fragrance for summer, for example, or a heavier version of a light fragrance for winter. But even flankers are not impervious to failure. At the end of the day, only the customer's nose knows best.

Spikes, strikes, swings and vamps

(Broadway Company Manager)

The hours are ridiculous, making a living is all but impossible, but those who work on the Great White Way will tell you that Broadway gets in your blood.

Part of it is the camaraderie of such an intensely collaborative environment. Some of it is that nightly rush of applause. But there is also, as one veteran show manager says, "the joy of knowing that you're doing this for real live people."

"I'm in the theater." You seldom hear theater people tell you precisely *where* in the theater they are, or which show they're associated with, or just what exactly it is that they do. It goes back to that being-in-your-blood thing. They may actually be between jobs (translation: out of work), but they'll be back. Which means they're still, in Broadway-speak, in the theater.

In the house. To theater folks, it's a house, not a theater.

One theory is because they spend more time there than in a traditional one. A Broadway house has at least 500 seats.

House left, stage right. Sailors and pilots use *port* and *starboard* to mark the sides of their craft. In a theater, your perspective depends on where you are: in the audience (the house) or on the stage. House left is the same as stage right, and stage left is the same as house right.

Deck. The stage, and an example of Broadway's borrowing a nautical term. While Broadway theaters have decks, not all theaters do. Those that don't are known as black box theaters.

Raked deck. A deck that's higher upstage (in the back) than downstage (in the front), often for the sight line or to force a perspective. When one actor is upstage of another, the actor who is upstage draws the audience's focus. Hence the figurative expression of being upstaged.

Fourth wall. The physical and psychological space between the stage and the audience. An environmental production is one where actors break the fourth wall and come into the audience. Shakespeare often staged such

Words At Work

productions in London's Globe Theatre, where the stage
jutted out into the audience.

Headers and legs. The stationary curtains that go across
the top of the stage are the headers. Those on either side are
the legs, which fly in and out. Legs hang directly behind the
proscenium, the arch that separates the house from the stage.

"Tab the curtain." Hold the leg open for an actor coming
onstage or going off.

House curtain. The curtain—often red
velvet—that opens and closes a performance.
Broadway shows are timed so carefully that it's
rare to have more than one curtain call except on
opening night. Union rules, folks: the show can't
run past 11:00 p.m.

Drops. The curtains behind the house curtain.
They're hung from long pipes and fly in and out.

House curtain

Painted drops have scenery painted on the fabric.

Flyman. The person in the wings who's in charge of
operating the drops, which come in from the fly space
directly over the stage.

Spike tape. The colored tape on the deck that tells an actor where to stand or the crew where to place a prop.

"He's at a load-out." For many years, before a show opened on Broadway, it went on tour to gauge audience reaction. Loading out a set meant dismantling it so you could take it to the next stop, where you would load in the set.

Strike the set. A phrase that strikes fear in the hearts of Broadway producers, it means dismantling the set for good. The show's finished.

Swings. The lowest paid of all the performers, these understudies to the chorus swing in and out of several parts. One night, the swing might be the third chorus girl from the left; the next night, the swing is the second from the right. A regular understudy is paid to fill a specific part. Swings, on the other hand, get paid for only one part in the chorus, even if they fill in for six different singers and dancers in the course of a show.

Standbys. The top-paid understudies who fill in for the stars of the show. They're not required to show up every night as long as they're nearby, but they're paid anyway and paid more if they do go on. Standbys are usually assigned to only those performers who are billed above the title on the theater's marquee.

Vamp. A few extra measures of music that an orchestra plays to give a performer time for additional applause, or for a long exit or entrance.

Triple threat. Someone who can sing, dance and act more than a little. Even on Broadway, a triple threat is rare.

Stage whisper. Not a whisper at all. It's a way of speaking that uses a lot of breath so that your voice projects into the theater and sounds like a (loud) whisper.

"Break a leg." It's bad luck in the theater to wish someone good luck; instead, say "break a leg" to performers before they go on and it won't happen.

Dark. On an internal schedule of show times, "dark" is listed next to the day that the theater is closed (hence, the stage is dark).

"It's a four-wall deal." An arrangement whereby a producer rents a theater and receives a package deal for use of the seats, house curtain, sprinklers and any other permanent installations (along with the four walls). Everything else, including office supplies, backstage and front-of-house staffs, and a lighting and sound package, is à la carte costs for the producer.

Papering the house. A way that producers make sure the seats are filled for a performance, especially when theater critics are scheduled to be there, by offering complimentary tickets. From a monetary standpoint, these freebies are worth only the paper they're printed on, since their revenue value is zero. Producers might also paper the house for a pre-opening night production so that the director and cast can gauge audience reactions.

Hardwood

House seats. Those reserved for the producers and creative team for each performance. If the seats aren't used, they're turned over to the box office to sell.

Daily wrap. The money a box office takes in each day. At

one time, the office staff wrapped cash in paper and rubber bands before taking it to the bank.

"What's our advance for the week?" How many sales have we made for upcoming performances? The advance is an important indicator of a show's success.

Hardwood. A paper ticket, in the days before computerized ticketing.

Deadwood. That same ticket, but the portion that the ticket taker tears off and the house keeps. The ticket becomes dead once the performance has taken place. Before computers, Broadway's bean counters counted deadwood as a way of verifying box office statements. Broadway may be the only place where deadwood is a sign that business is good.

"Do it in the hood"

(Microbiologist)

As one member of this profession observed, "I've never known a microbiologist yet who ate sushi." You might not eat it, either, if you studied a micro world of bacteria, viruses and fungi. There could be parasites or other bugs in that raw fish—and not the creepy-crawly bugs you're probably thinking of. Bugs vs. true bugs. *Bugs* is shorthand for bacteria or viruses. These are the bugs that might be in that sushi. *True bugs* is the term for certain insects, those within the order *Hemiptera*. They tend to have wings, like to bite and age gradually if not always gracefully. The rest of those creepy-crawlies may bug you, but technically they're only insects.

Grasshoppers, ants and fleas are insects. Cicadas, aphids and bed bugs are true bugs.

(*Good night, sleep tight, don't let the Hemiptera bite.*)

True bug

Words At Work

Spray & pray. Sick plants don't surrender their secrets easily. Plant diseases can take a confoundingly long time to pinpoint. Meanwhile, the grass on the golf course is wasting away. Often the stop-gap solution is to make an educated guess at what may be causing the problem and to apply a pesticide, without knowing specifically what pest it is you're trying to control. You spray the pesticide and pray that it works.

Nozzlehead. The one spraying and praying and applying the pesticide. If the pesticide in question is especially toxic, the nozzlehead is smart to suit up in a spray suit. This protective clothing is made of a lightweight material that's impermeable to chemicals.

One for the pot, not. If two tablespoons of a pesticide work well, won't three work even better? No, exhort plant specialists, who try to break consumers' habit of overdosing their sick plants by adding "one for the pot." That's best left to brewing tea, where it's customary to use one teaspoon per cup and then to add one more to the teapot.

Microbiologist

Gene jockey. A scientist who manipulates a microorganism's genes by removing a piece of DNA from one microorganism and placing it into another. Gregor Mendel, the famous nineteenth-century botanist, manipulated on the macro level, with seeds and pollens. Gene jockeys scale it to the micro level, with DNA. Cloning is just one aspect of this kind of genetic engineering. Gene expression is another—finding how a gene functions and what it produces.

Splicing & dicing. Chefs chop vegetables; gene jockeys chop DNA. Instead of a knife, scientists use either enzymes or a sonic method, much like the process used to clean jewelry. Once sliced, the DNA can be spliced, or manipulated.

Subbing and streaking. If you're subbing, you're sub-culturing, or purifying, mixed cultures of bacteria. When you're streaking, you're separating and diluting a small amount of that mixed culture in the hopes of getting a single bacterial colony.

"Suck it up." One of the staples of a microbiologist's lab is pipettes. Tubes of glass or plastic, they allow you to pick up and dispense a precise volume of the liquid you're using to create the media, or food source, that helps the microbe you're studying to grow on its Petri dish. To bring the liquid into the pipette, you have to literally suck it up. But prudent scientists realize that it's best not to inhale, so they don't pipette by mouth—or at least, they don't admit to it. Instead, they use a rubber bulb on the end of the pipette. Or they take no chances at all and use automatic pumps.

Hockey stick. Venture capitalists aren't the only ones partial to hockey sticks. Microbiologists use their equivalent when they're spreading a microbe-containing extract onto the media in a Petri dish. The L-shaped glass rod that helps to distribute the material evenly across the media surface is the hockey stick.

Plating the sample. Much the way a chef artfully arranges food on a plate, a microbiologist plates the Petri dish with the microbial extract, adding a food source to help the organism grow. Alas, sometimes the reaction is the same as a displeased chef's with an underling's failed concoction, with the microbiologist announcing that "there's nothing but

Microbiologist

garbage on this plate." Everything grew in the Petri dish except the bug that the scientist was seeking.

"Do it in the hood." To ensure a sterile environment, microbiologists pour the media into the Petri dish inside a hood. The hood resembles a box with one side missing and serves as a biological safety cabinet, with an air filter that screens out contaminants on both sides of the box. There's room inside the hood for scientists to get their hands in, but nothing more. Which also helps protect them from being exposed to some of the very microorganisms they love to study.

"You're the stick in this trick"

(Magician)

Those who practice magic aspire to more than merely fooling us. The good ones leave you so entertained that, for a Merlin moment at least, you're content to utterly surrender to the experience.

Unlike other professions, magic has no formal place of study and awards no degree. But through training courses, conventions and trade associations, you can learn some of the craft behind the art. And there's no magic involved in buying tricks: hundreds are developed and sold every year.

Box jumper. How many women get to include on their résumés that they're pros at appearing and disappearing from boxes? Women who are sawn in two, an illusion that a British magician introduced in the late 1800s, are the classic box jumpers.

Zigzag lady. This time the woman gets to stay in one

piece, but talk about a stretch—as she stands in a narrow cabinet, the magician "zigs" her torso one way while the rest of her "zags" the other. Don't try this in your yoga class.

Zombie. You might think it's what box jumpers and zigzag ladies eventually become, but a zombie is a ball that appears to float beneath, beside and on top of a large silken cloth that the magician holds outstretched.

"That trick has bad angles." Angles are sight lines, which give the audience the opportunity to see the *aha!* behind the abracadabra. To compensate, a magician performs the trick only in certain settings, such as a theater, where audience members can see only what happens directly in front of them. If, on the other hand, the trick is angleproof, the audience can surround the stage (or the magician).

"The effect was terrific, and I didn't reveal the secret." The effect is what the audience sees. The secret is the method the magician uses to perform the trick. One of the secrets to not revealing the secret is to light the trick correctly, which in magic means so that the audience can't see your method.

Words At Work

Flashing. "I did some beautiful effects, but I flashed a couple of them," a magician might say ruefully. Nothing pornographic about this flashing, but the magician did inadvertently expose some of the secrets.

Sucker trick. When the magician appears to share the secret with the audience, or the audience seems to catch on to how it's done, it's just a different kind of illusion. Here's a sucker trick that works like a charm:

Mr. Magician waves a silk handkerchief and it turns into an egg. But then he confesses that it's not a real egg, and to prove it he pulls the silk handkerchief out of the egg's wooden shell. At the same time, he's pulled the wool over your eyes. The next thing you know, he's breaking the shell from what you thought was a wooden egg and...it's a real egg after all.

Talking. The magician's conversation with the audience (yes, it's a distraction device) is more correctly called patter. Talking is what coins do—but in this case, it's not good that money talks. It means that the two coins you palmed, or concealed in your hand, inadvertently hit each other and clinked, or talked.

In palming, your legerdemain can take two forms. In a front palm, the audience sees the back of your hand; in a back palm, the audience sees the front. A back palm is more difficult because you're showing more of your hand.

Miser's dream. The trick that
produces money from thin air.
Dream on.

Miser's dream

"You're the stick in this trick."

Congratulations: you've been conscripted as the confederate in the audience, also known as the stooge or the shill. You are, in other words, posing as an audience member while you're really there to help the magician pull off a trick.

Misdirection. Distracting the audience so that they're
focusing on something else while the magician accomplishes the secret. The stick in the trick might be part of a misdirection.

Performing in one. Performing in front of the curtain, as
in a variety show, when the curtain has to close in preparation for the next act.

Cardician. A specialist in card tricks.

Asrah. Defying gravity is one of the tricks of the magician trade, and there are different ways to do it. One is suspension, where you float in mid-air without moving up and down. In levitation, you do move up and down at the magician's command. Now levitate while under a cloth, and when the magician pulls the cloth away...*poof!* You've vanished into thin air. That's an Asrah. The name is a fanciful concoction that its inventor, a magician named LeRoy, pulled out of thin air.

Underground magic. Sorcery so sophisticated, only a few of the very best conjurers know about it. Underground magic is never publicized. Even those who make magic can fall under its spell.

Final Word

First, about that quiz at the beginning of the book: the answers are 1j, 2d, 3b, 4a, 5k, 6g, 7i, 8l, 9o, 10e or m, 11n, 12h, 13c, 14m, 15p, 16f.

If you're wondering where the hairdresser's torn & tattered came from (16f), you'll find it online, along with more coinages of *coiffeurs* such as walking & talking and shifts, stacks and feathers. Visit www.walkerbooks.com.

As for the final word, it's two: big ears. The expression, when made about musicians, is a compliment. It means that they're so attuned to their craft, they can hear a piece of music once and play it back without missing a beat—or a note.

Big ears is also a trait of word lovers, whose ears are fine-tuned to the nuances of language. We've already begun our list of terms and professions for the next edition of *Words At Work*. If you have a professions expression that you'd like to share, please email us at feedback@bloomsburyusa.com. We're all ears.

Humanography
(A living bibliography)

Rather than reading an assortment of books, listening to professionals well versed in their craft served as the primary research for this book. And so instead of a bibliography, here is a humanography.

Nancy Barbery has been a professional hair stylist since 1975 and has owned and operated a full-service salon in South Florida. She is licensed in both New York and Florida and has received extensive training from the Redken Exchange in New York City. She is a graduate of Ultissima Beauty Institute in New York.

Kimberly R. Carmen, a Registered Pharmacist in Florida and Illinois, has been a retail pharmacist and pharmacy manager since 1983. She also has served as director of pharmacy operations for Caremark, a mail-order pharmaceutical firm.

Humanography

She holds a B.S. in Pharmacy from the Drake University College of Pharmacy.

Michael Chambers is a veteran of both the stage and the restaurant kitchen. A former member of the Old Vic Theatre School in Bristol, England, he was also the stage manager for the New York Shakespeare Festival Public Theater. He worked as a prep chef and kitchen manager in restaurants on Fire Island for seven years. He holds a B.A. in Drama from Goddard College.

Jo Ann Chism has worked as a writer and producer of television promotions since 1993. She began her career at local news affiliates and then moved to national cable networks, MSNBC and Lifetime Television among them. She holds a B.A. in Radio and Television from the University of Central Florida.

Maureen Dobuski first came to Consolidated Drake Press in Philadelphia as a customer. She was so impressed, she joined the printing company in 1985. In addition to being the vice president of sales and marketing, she is now one of the company principals. She holds a B.A. from St. Joseph's University.

Monica Elliott is a professor of plant pathology at the University of Florida, where she has been on the faculty since 1987. A member of the American Society for Microbiology, she holds an M.S. and a Ph.D. in Plant Pathology from Montana State University. She also earned a J.D. from Nova Southeastern University and is a member of the Florida Bar.

John B. Frick is a general partner of Chisholm Private Capital and was the founder of Argo Ventures, both venture capital firms. A Certified Public Accountant, he has held executive positions in the investment and financial arenas since 1985. He earned his M.B.A. from the Stanford University Graduate School of Business.

Humanography

Paul F. Gehl heads the John M. Wing Foundation on the
History of Printing at the Newberry Library in Chicago, where
he has worked since 1984. A member of the Early Book
Society, he has written numerous scholarly works on the
printing methods for books during the Renaissance and is a
contributor to the *Dictionary of Literary Biography*. Both his
M.A. and Ph.D. in History are from the University of Chicago.

Brent Graef has been in the hotel industry all his life. He
grew up in hotels, as his father was in the business, and has
worked in them since 1991. He has served in management
capacities for Four Seasons properties since 2000, at both
the Four Seasons Resort Palm Beach and the Regent Beverly
Wilshire. He earned a bachelor's in business administration
from Florida International University.

Bob Hovan has been in sales and management positions with
RR Donnelley, the largest printer in North America, since
1978. He holds a B.S. in Industry and Technology from
Northern Illinois University.

Humanography

Brad Lucas is a partner in Anton Lucas Inc., an investment banking firm based in Boston that specializes in merger and acquisition assignments. He has held positions in banking and finance since 1984. His M.B.A. is from the Wharton School of the University of Pennsylvania. He also studied at the London School of Economics.

Bert Luer is the managing partner of a waste transfer and recycling facility in South Florida. He has worked in management positions in the waste industry since 1984 and spearheaded the launch of Waste Management Inc.'s residential and commercial recycling programs throughout Florida. He holds a master's in urban and regional planning from the University of Florida.

J. Anthony Magner has been in the theater since 1981, working on and off Broadway. He has been company manager for such productions as *Cats, Annie Get Your Gun* and *Requiem*, and has handled national and international tours of shows such as *Les Misérables*. He was the first manager of the Off-Broadway Dodger Stages before moving to London to work on productions there. He is a graduate of the University of Massachusetts at Amherst.

Rich McFeaters has been a research scientist at Kraft Inc. since 1979, primarily in the Nabisco Biscuit Snack & Confection division. He is responsible for developing Ritz Bits, Teddy Grahams and SnackWell's product lines for the North American market as well as new cookies in the European market. He holds five patents for product and process design. He earned a B.S. in Food Science from the Pennsylvania State University and is a member of the university's Food Science Task Force.

Peter Meade is the president of Phase Two Funds LLC, a real estate consulting and investment company. A retailer since 1971, he has served as a regional vice president for The Limited and as vice president of retail stores for Polo Ralph Lauren. He also provides project management services for new retail properties, from design and construction to fixturing and merchandising.

Humanography

Larry Owsowitz made his first solo flight on his sixteenth birthday. He flew F-16s more than 2,500 hours in Europe, Asia and the Americas while a pilot in the U. S. Air Force. A copilot for American Airlines since 1993, he flies Boeing 767s internationally, logging approximately a half million miles a year.

Leif Peterson began his retail career in 1985 with one of the country's legendary department stores, Marshall Field's (now Macy's). He is its senior business manager of partner businesses. He holds a B.A. from the University of Mary.

Gene Pokorny has been principal tuba of the Chicago Symphony Orchestra since 1989. He has served in this capacity for the Los Angeles Philharmonic, the St. Louis Symphony, the Utah Symphony and the Israel Philharmonic. He is a graduate of the University of Southern California, with a bachelor's in music performance.

Humanography

Robert J. Simonelli has been a partner and general manager of the Landing Restaurant and Pub in Marblehead, Massachusetts, since 2001. He has been in the restaurant trade since the 1970s, with stints as dishwasher, cook, bartender and waiter. He has worked in management capacities at establishments in Laguna Beach, Palm Springs and Boston. He is, he says, in school every day in the restaurant business—always learning.

Thomas S. Skrobacz is the manager of supply chain finance for Elizabeth Arden Inc. His launch work for European and American markets has included the Elizabeth Taylor and Elizabeth Arden fragrance lines. He holds a bachelor's in business administration from St. Bonaventure University and an M.B.A. from Sacred Heart University.

Sahar Swidan, who holds a doctorate in pharmacy from the University of Michigan, is the CEO and founder of Pharmacy Solutions, a retail pharmacy in Michigan that specializes in personalized medicine. She also serves as the CEO of

Humanography

NeuroPharmacology Consultants and is a clinical associate professor of pharmacy at the University of Michigan in Ann Arbor. She is a Board Certified Pharmacotherapy Specialist.

Roberta Tankanow is a Registered Pharmacist in Michigan and is a clinical associate professor of pharmacy at the University of Michigan in Ann Arbor. She has also been a clinical pharmacist for the university since 1977, during which time she instituted an Investigational Drug Service for coordinating the university's drug studies. She holds a B.S. in Pharmacy from Northeastern University and an M.S. in Hospital Pharmacy from Wayne State University.

Leigh Tunney spent twenty years in the restaurant trade, working in establishments in Hawaii, Ohio and Washington, running the gamut from fast food to fine dining. In addition to management positions she has been bartender, caterer, prep cook, baker, busser and dishwasher. Her current venture is a café specializing in organic foods. She holds a degree in English from Seattle University.

Humanography

Wayne J. Welch, a captain with American Airlines since 1986, has logged more than 10,000 flight hours piloting the Boeing 727, 757 and 767. He flies both domestic and international routes, including Europe, the Caribbean and Central America. He received his flight training in the U.S. Navy, flying the P-3 Orion for Patrol Squadron Fifty in the Pacific, Alaska and Far East. His B.A. is from Harvard.

Mark Wilson is considered one of the top ten American magicians of the twentieth century and is an inductee into the Magician's Hall of Fame. He starred in the first weekly magic series on network television, *The Magic Land of Allakazam,* and has schooled such celebrities as Johnny Carson, Cary Grant and Cher in the art of magic. He has designed entertainment packages for leading theme parks, including Disneyland, and is the author of the world's bestselling book of magic instruction, *Mark Wilson's Complete Course in Magic.*

Gerald T. Zoppi has worked in the hospitality industry since 1976. Many of these years have been in management capacities for the Hotels of Distinction group, including the job of conference manager for the Copley Plaza in Boston. He has also worked for the Konover Hotel Corporation. He holds a B.A. from St. Bonaventure University.

Other professionals who contributed their expertise include David Brown, Roger Horchow and Jonathan Levine (Broadway); Marcie Wallen (hairdresser); John Armato (magician); Eric Boa, James C. Fuscoe III and Nigel Harrison (microbiologist); Vic Vena (pharmacist); Adam Grant and Rick Sparkes (printer); Don Sturdy (restaurateur); Joe Aronstein, Ray Moore and Frank Weissman (retailer); Wendy Koons (symphony orchestra musician); Russell Grant (television promo producer); and Cynthia Fisher, Jim Koch, Wendy Phillips, Suzette Recinos and Pam Robertson (venture capitalist).

Sources for examples cited in the Introduction include Ron Ash (engineer), Gerald Madeiras (industrial plumber), Ronald L. Book (lobbyist) and Mitch Gordon (police).

Sources of Help, Hope and Inspiration

My thanks to the friends who helped connect me to pros, especially Carmen Ayala, Eric Chism, Larry and Sue Ford, Megan Gordon and Jon Phillips. Those who volunteer to read manuscripts provide a service above and beyond the call of friendship. John Armato offered time he didn't have and the creative thinking that only he could give. I was also fortunate to have Rita Keiser, Larry Jenkins, Kathryn Messier and Jim Mustich as readers. Bob Greenman was an ever-helpful resource on questions of etymology.

Dee Moustakas performed her multiple roles of editor, adviser, sounding board and friend with her customary engagement and generosity. Luise Erdmann brought clarity and red ink wherever it was needed. The Levenger Press gang—Vicki Ehrenman, Danielle Furci, Tina St. Pierre and lifetime member Jeff Simon—was as persnickety as always in delivering a professional, polished product to the printer.

Sources of Help, Hope and Inspiration

Lee Passarella's extraordinary artistic talent turned a book about sayings into a book that sings.

Paul Dickson and George Gibson helped this book take its first steps and were so gracious in doing so. Peg Fradette, Mercedes Lawry, Carolyn Martine, Andrea Syverson and my mother, Martha Guson, offered the magic ingredient in soldiering on: encouragement.

To Steve and Lori Leveen, my thanks for the support you give writers and their readers. And to Jodi R. R. Smith, who was the first to see this book's possibilities, you have my everlasting gratitude.

About the Creators

The author

Mim Harrison has been a speechwriter, scriptwriter and ghostwriter for numerous professions since 1984. She is the founding editor of Levenger Press and has written pieces on Winston Churchill, Robert Louis Stevenson and Alexis de Tocqueville for the imprint's titles. She is also the creator of an online column on the reading habits of writers. A graduate of Allegheny College, she has also studied at the University of Hull, England.

The artist

A native of New York City's Greenwich Village, Lee Passarella received her formal training in art at Pratt Institute and The New School. She pursued post-graduate courses in various artistic media and has worked primarily in watercolors since 1995. She is the illustrator of the bestselling book *Rare Words* in addition to being a product designer. Her portfolio can be viewed at Leepassarella.com.

Index of Terms

A

B

Index of Terms

Index of Terms

Index of Terms

Index of Terms

Index of Terms

Index of Terms

Index of Terms

P

packers 73

page was black, the 58

painted drops 84

papering the house 87

pax 20

penny stacking xi, 29

perfect bound 54

performing in one 97

piggyback 66

pile it high, watch it fly 12

planogram 12

plant it 22

plating the sample 92

plug 51

poodle traffic 11

POOS 81

popping 'em 14

post 42

power back 17

practicing polypharmacy 33

precon 46

prestige channel 78

price point 12

printer's devil 51

process colors 53

protocept 25

pucks xi, 77

pushing the tempo 60

putrescible 70

PWP 15

R

racks 45

rain catcher 57

raked deck 83

ramps 18

read 40

red-bag waste 73

Index of Terms

Index of Terms

Index of Terms

T

U

Index of Terms

ups 4

upstage 83

V

vamp 86

variant 81

view tables 2

vintage year 64, 69

Vitamin R 34

Vitamin V 34

VO 40, 44

vulture capitalists 68

W

walk 48

walking & talking 99

walking business 13

wand wagger xiv, 57

waste stream 73

we have a double
rehearsal today 58

weather 20

weeping marshmallows 26

whale 8

what's our advance for
the week? 88

white flash 42

white good 71

who's your nose? 76

widows 52

wing walkers 23

wire choir 57

working with riddles 32

Y

yard wastes 71

you have a squatter at sixteen 2

you need to color it up 37

you need to woodshed that 61

you're the stick in this trick 97

Z

zigzag lady 94

zombie 66, 95

Uncommon Books
for Serious Readers

Boston
Henry Cabot Lodge

A Boy at the Hogarth Press
Written and illustrated by
Richard Kennedy

The Dream
Sir Winston Churchill

Feeding the Mind
Lewis Carroll

A Fortnight in the Wilderness
Alexis de Tocqueville

The Little Guide to Your
Well-Read Life
Steve Leveen

New York
Theodore Roosevelt

On a Life Well Spent
Cicero
Preface by Benjamin Franklin

Painting as a Pastime
Winston S. Churchill

Rare Words
Jan Leighton and Hallie Leighton

The Silverado Squatters
Six selected chapters
Robert Louis Stevenson

Words That Make a Difference
Robert Greenman

Levenger Press is the publishing arm of

LEVENGER®
TOOLS FOR SERIOUS READERS

Levenger.com   **800.544.0880**